SCHOLASTIC

PIONEER
~*~ Mini-Books ~*~

12 Reproducible Comic Book-Style Stories That Introduce Kids to the Westward Movement—and Motivate All Readers

by Sarah Glasscock

New York • Toronto • London • Auckland • Sydney
Mexico City • New Delhi • Hong Kong • Buenos Aires

Teaching Resources

Scholastic Inc. grants teachers permission to photocopy the mini-book pages for classroom use. No other part of this publication may be reproduced in whole or in part, or stored in a retrieval system, or transmitted in any form or by any means, electronic, mechanical, photocopying, recording, or otherwise, without written permission of the publisher. For information regarding permission, write to Scholastic Inc., 557 Broadway, New York, NY 10012.

Cover and interior design by Kelli Thompson
Cover and interior illustrations by Michelle Dorenkamp

ISBN 0-439-31751-7
Copyright © 2004 by Sarah Glasscock
All rights reserved.
Printed in the U.S.A.

1 2 3 4 5 6 7 8 9 10   40   10 09 08 07 06 05 04

CONTENTS

INTRODUCTION 4

1775: Daniel Boone and the Wilderness Road 7

1804: Lewis & Clark's Corps of Discovery 13

1806: Mountain Men 19

1820: Americans in Texas 25

1838: Trail of Tears 31

1843: Oregon Trail 37

1849: California Gold Rush 43

1860: Pony Express 49

1862: Homesteaders on the Great Plains 55

1866: Cattle Drives 61

1869: Transcontinental Railroad 67

1886: Geronimo and the Closing of the West 73

INTRODUCTION

A pioneer is defined as someone who goes before and opens up or prepares the way for others to follow. American pioneers moved west for a variety of reasons:

- In the 19th century, the United States population was increasing rapidly due to high birth rates and immigration. Agriculture was still the main means of support; large families were necessary to work farms.
- More land was needed, and land on the frontier was inexpensive or, in some cases, free.
- The frontier opened commercial opportunities and the possibility for individual advancement.
- The United States experienced depressions in 1818 and in 1839, influencing some people to try to earn their living in the West.
- Ports on the West Coast could expand U.S. trade to China, Japan, and other Pacific countries.
- Some Southerners hoped to increase the slave-holding territories of the U.S. by expanding West.
- Americans hoped to put a stop to British expansion on the West Coast.

In the 1840s, American politicians such as Thomas Hart Benton began using the phrase "manifest destiny" to describe, defend, and encourage the United States's westward expansion. They said it was America's duty to expand its territory and spread democracy. Native Americans and other non-Europeans, however, were deemed to be incapable of self-government and participating in democracy.

HOW TO USE THIS BOOK

The 12 mini-books in this book focus on American pioneers during the 19th century, beginning with Daniel Boone and the opening of the West with the Wilderness Trail. The last mini-book ends with the capture of Geronimo and the closing of the West.

Presented in a comic-book format with illustrations and easy text, these mini-books are designed to engage readers at all levels. They encourage students to delve more deeply into the mass movement west—its benefits and consequences—that shaped our country.

Each mini-book is preceded by teacher pages that include the following sections:

COVER

For students to color and cut out for their mini-books

BACKGROUND

A historical overview of the topic. This background material is written for you, the teacher, so you can decide on the best way to present the information to your students. A fun fact appears at the end of the background material.

VOCABULARY

Lists potentially difficult or unfamiliar words that appear in each mini-book. These words are introduced once in the mini-books in which they appear. You may also want to pronounce the names of people and locations in each mini-book for students before they begin reading.

RESOURCES

Includes books and Web sites that students might enjoy exploring

ACTIVITIES

Four activities that reinforce and extend the topic. These activities are cross-curricular and focus on discussion, writing, and research.

HOW TO MAKE THE MINI-BOOKS

1. Carefully tear along the perforation to remove the mini-book pages you want to use. Make double-sided photocopies of the mini-book pages.

   *** NOTE:** If your photocopy machine does not have a double-sided function, follow these directions:
   - First, make copies of the first full page of the mini-book (pages 1 and 3).
   - Place these copies in the paper tray with the blank side facing up.
   - Next, make a copy of the second full page of the mini-book (pages 2 and 4) so that the page copies directly behind mini-book pages 1 and 3.
   - Make a test copy to be sure the pages are aligned correctly and that mini-book page 2 appears directly behind mini-book page 1.
   - Repeat these steps for pages 5 and 7, and 6 and 8.

2. Photocopy and cut out the cover for the mini-book from the teacher pages.

3. Cut the double-sided mini-book pages along the dashed lines.

4. Place the pages in numerical order, and then staple them along the mini-book's spine.

☞1775☜
DANIEL BOONE AND THE WILDERNESS ROAD

BACKGROUND

Frontiersman Daniel Boone helped open up the territory beyond the original 13 colonies for settlement. He was born in the fall of 1734 to a Pennsylvania Quaker family. As a child, Daniel spent time with the Delaware Indians in the region and learned outdoor skills from them. He had no formal schooling, but a sister-in-law taught him to read and write.

Between 1769 and 1771, Daniel first explored Kentucky. Two years later, he led a group of settlers, including his own family, to Kentucky. The expedition failed when Indians attacked and killed members of a small supply party, including James Boone, Daniel's son. In 1775 Daniel was hired to create the Wilderness Road out of existing Native American and buffalo trails. He established Fort Boone, renamed Boonesborough, at the end of the road.

Although King George III had issued the Proclamation of 1763, forbidding settlement west of the Allegheny Mountains, Boone and other English settlers ignored the ban. He brought his family and others to Boonesborough. Despite dwindling supplies and confrontations with Shawnee, Cherokee, Delaware, and Mingo tribes in the region, the settlement endured. Daniel Boone, however, suffered bad luck. He was robbed of $20,000 when he went to Virginia to buy land warrants for Kentucky settlers. His son, Israel, was killed at the Battle of Blue Licks.

Daniel moved his family to various places in Kentucky and West Virginia. In 1799 they moved to Missouri. Daniel lived to see the region become a United States territory as part of the Louisiana Purchase. He died on September 26, 1820.

IN FACT... Daniel never wore a coonskin cap. He braided his long hair or twisted it in a knot and smeared it with bear grease.

VOCABULARY

Introduce or review the following words: *preferred, control, support, treaty, convinced, surrender, settler, wounded.*

Before students begin to read, you may want to pronounce the names of people and places that appear in the mini-book.

RESOURCES

BOOKS:
My Father, Daniel Boone: The Draper Interviews with Nathan Boone
   edited by Neal O. Hammon (University Press of Kentucky, 1999)
Daniel Boone: Frontier Legend
   by Pat McCarthy (Enslow, 2000)

INTERNET:
Archiving Early America
   http://earlyamerica.com/lives/boone/index.html
American West: Daniel Boone
   http://www.americanwest.com/pages/boone.htm

ACTIVITIES

A DASH OF SALT: The settlers at Boonesborough made their own salt by boiling water from salt springs. Bring in different kinds of salt, such as kosher, sea, and iodized salt for students to examine and compare. Invite students to research various ways in which salt is processed today. To enrich the activity, help students make salt as the settlers did. Dissolve a liberal amount of salt in a pan of water. Boil the water until salt forms on the sides of the pan.

MAPPING BOONE: The first settlement to be named after Daniel Boone was Fort Boone. Since then, many places have been named after the frontiersman. Challenge pairs of students to find places on a U.S. map with Boone in their names. In which states did they find the most places named after Boone?

FRIENDS AND FOES: Delaware Indians first taught Boone about the outdoors. In Florida, the Seminole helped him. And although Boone often fought the Shawnee and Cherokee, he also had friends in both tribes. Divide the class into four groups. Ask each group to find out more about one of the Indian tribes Daniel Boone interacted with. How have each tribe's fortunes changed since the 1700s?

THE FRENCH AND INDIAN WAR: Daniel Boone drove a supply wagon during the French and Indian War. Give each student a different topic about the French and Indian War to research; for example, George Washington and Fort Necessity, Fort Duquesne, Chief Pontiac, the battles of Brushy Run and Quebec, Joseph Brant, the Treaty of Paris, and the Proclamation of 1763. Have students present their findings in chronological order. You might also want to have them create a time line of the war based on their presentations.

Daniel Boone was born in 1734 in Pennsylvania. He spent most of his time outdoors, where he learned how to track animals and build shelters from the Delaware Indians who lived in the woods nearby.

One night, when he was about 13 years old, Daniel didn't return home. His mother Sarah was afraid he had gotten lost. She asked neighbors to help her search for Daniel.

⭐ 1 ⭐

After returning from the war, Daniel fell in love with his neighbor, Rebecca Bryan. Daniel showed up at the Bryan's house with a deer he had killed. Rebecca then cooked the deer meat.

Daniel and Rebecca were married in 1756. Several years later Daniel heard about free land in Florida. He explored the area but found few animals to hunt. Still, Daniel tried to talk Rebecca into moving there.

⭐ 3 ⭐

The Boones left Pennsylvania in 1750 and settled in North Carolina. Although Daniel helped his father Squire in the fields, he preferred hunting and trapping in the woods.

In 1755, France and England battled for control of North America. Many Indian tribes supported France because they were angry that England had taken their land. Daniel drove a supply wagon for the British.

From 1769 to 1772, Daniel explored Kentucky. He hunted buffalo and had some run-ins with Shawnee Indians. They didn't want white settlers moving into the area and taking land.

The King of England proclaimed that nobody could settle land west of the Appalachian Mountains. Daniel tried to change that in 1773. He led a group of people, including his family, to Kentucky.

Daniel's son and others were killed by Delaware, Shawnee, and Cherokee Indians. Most of the settlers decided to return to North Carolina. Fighting continued between whites and Indians until a treaty was signed. Daniel helped build a road so white settlers could move into Kentucky.

5

In early 1778, Daniel led some men to salt springs near Boonesborough. While the other men boiled the water to make salt, Daniel hunted. A group of Shawnee captured Daniel.

Daniel convinced his men at the salt springs to surrender. They were adopted by the Shawnee. Soon Chief Blackfish trusted Daniel. Because of this, he was able to escape and return home.

7

At the end of Wilderness Road, Daniel chose a spot on the Kentucky River. A fort and cabins were built. In 1775 Daniel brought his family to the place, which was called Boonesborough.

Life in Boonesborough wasn't easy. Problems arose between the settlers and Mingo, Shawnee, and Cherokee Indians. In the summer of 1776, Indians kidnapped Daniel's daughter, Jemima, and two other girls. He rescued them.

✯ **6** ✯

A Shawnee war party with over 400 men soon attacked Boonesborough. For more than 11 days the settlers held them off. Daniel was wounded in the shoulder.

Daniel and Rebecca moved several more times. In 1799, they finally settled in Missouri. Long after Daniel's death in 1820, pioneers continued to travel west on the Wilderness Road.

✯ **8** ✯

1804
LEWIS & CLARK'S CORPS OF DISCOVERY

BACKGROUND

On February 28, 1803, President Thomas Jefferson received Congressional approval to send an expedition to explore the land west of the Mississippi River. In addition to learning about the region's Native American groups, geography, and plants and animals, he hoped to find the Northwest Passage to the Pacific Ocean and gain a foothold in the fur trade in the French-owned Louisiana Territory. Jefferson asked his personal secretary, Captain Meriwether Lewis, to lead the expedition. At Lewis's request, Jefferson tapped William Clark as co-captain. When the United States purchased the Louisiana Territory from France on April 30, 1803, the expedition's mission expanded. Lewis would also have to let the Indian tribes in the region know that the territory had changed hands. The expedition encountered almost 50 different Native American tribes.

The Corps of Discovery consisted of 33 members—white, black, Indian, and racially mixed—including Sacagawea, a Shoshone woman, and York, an African-American slave who accompanied Clark. There was only one casualty on the trip; Charles Floyd died of what was probably a burst appendix.

The expedition set off from Camp Wood (also known as Camp Dubois) above St. Louis on the Mississippi River on May 14, 1804. On September 23, 1806, the Corps of Discovery returned to St. Louis. All the men received double pay and land. Lewis became governor of the new Louisiana Territory, but he committed suicide in 1809. Clark served as Indian agent for the West and brigadier general of the militia in the new territory. In 1812, after Sacagawea died, Clark raised her two children—Jean Baptiste (Pompey), who was born on the expedition, and Lisette.

IN FACT... The Lewis and Clark expedition cost a total of $38,722.

VOCABULARY

Introduce or review the following words: *discovery, woolly mammoth, purchase, territory, accompany, reckon, peaceful, coyotes, antelopes, prairie dogs, expedition, enormous, grizzly bear, gigantic, scout, landmarks, kidnapped, stumble, vote, household, celebrated, monsters*.

Before students begin to read, you may want to pronounce the names of people and places in the mini-book.

RESOURCES

BOOKS:

Bold Journey
by Charles Bohner (Houghton Mifflin, 1990)

Sacagawea: The Story of Bird Woman and the Lewis and Clark Expedition
by Joseph Bruchac (Scholastic, 2001)

Seaman: The Dog Who Explored the West With Lewis and Clark
by Gail Langer Karwoski (Peachtree Publishers, 1999)

Off the Map: The Journals of Lewis and Clark
edited by Connie and Peter Roop (Walker & Company, 1998)

INTERNET:

Journals of Lewis and Clark
http://xroads.virginia.edu/~HYPER/JOURNALS/journals.html

PBS Online—Lewis & Clark
http://www.pbs.org/lewisandclark

Traveler's Guide to the Lewis and Clark Trail
http://www.lewisandclark.com

ACTIVITIES

NORTHWEST PASSAGE: Thomas Jefferson hoped that Lewis and Clark would find a northwest passage across the country—a river passage from the Atlantic to the Pacific. Ask pairs of students to study world maps and then chart an eastern water route from Boston to China. If the Corps of Discovery had found a northwest passage, how would that have affected American trade with China?

EVERY MAP TELLS A STORY: Provide a time line of the Lewis and Clark expedition (from the PBS Web site) or journal entries written by members of the expedition. Then have groups of students use the information to make their own story maps about the expedition.

AN IMPORTANT VOTE: Although Sacagawea and York voted with the rest of the Corps of Discovery about where to spend the winter of 1805, it was many years before women, Native Americans, and African Americans won the right to vote. Guide students to find out more about the history of suffrage for women, Native Americans, and African Americans. Discuss how the United States might be different if certain groups of people weren't allowed to vote.

ON TODAY'S DATE: Read excerpts from Lewis and Clark's journals to students. What kinds of details did they find most striking in the entries, and why? Challenge students to keep their own journals for a week. Ask them to include observations and descriptions—even drawings—that would help people 200 years from now understand what life was like in the past.

In 1801, two-thirds of Americans lived within 50 miles of the Atlantic Ocean. The United States stretched west to the Mississippi River. The French owned most of the land beyond the river.

President Thomas Jefferson was curious about the rest of North America. He asked Meriwether Lewis to explore the land all the way to the Pacific Ocean. Then in 1803, France sold the land to the U.S. This was the Louisiana Purchase.

⋆ 1 ⋆

The men saw animals they'd never seen before—coyotes, antelopes, and prairie dogs. In the fall, they reached the villages of the Hidatsa and Mandan Indians. Lewis and Clark decided to stop there for the winter.

Two people joined the expedition—a fur trader named Toussaint Charbonneau and his Shoshone wife, Sacagawea. Although Sacagawea was pregnant, Lewis and Clark knew she would be able to help them.

⋆ 3 ⋆

In May 1804, the Corps of Discovery sailed up the Missouri River. Almost 40 men, a dog, and supplies were loaded into three boats. Sometimes they had to paddle or use ropes to pull the boats.

In August, Lewis and Clark met with a group of Oto and Missouri Indians. They handed out medals and American flags and made speeches.

★ 2 ★

In the spring of 1805, the expedition began moving west again. The sight of huge herds of buffalo amazed everyone. Then Lewis and another man met and killed an enormous grizzly bear.

That summer they came to a fork in the Missouri River. Lewis scouted along the south fork to figure out which way to go.

★ 4 ★

Carrying her baby, Sacagawea soon began to recognize landmarks. They were getting close to Shoshone territory. Scouting ahead again, Lewis climbed a mountain—and saw more mountains.

The rest of the expedition joined Lewis at a Shoshone village. Suddenly Sacagawea cried out. The chief of the village was her brother Cameahwait.

★ 5 ★

In November 1805, the expedition reached the Pacific Ocean. They had traveled over 4,000 miles! Lewis and Clark held a vote to decide where they should settle for the winter.

Meanwhile, a group of Missouri, Oto, Arikara, and Yankton Sioux chiefs visited Washington, D.C. They had met Lewis and Clark when the explorers passed through their territories.

★ 7 ★

The expedition left the village with Old Toby, a Shoshone guide, 29 horses, and one mule. They lost the trail in the Bitterroot Mountains. Snow began to fall, and they were short on supplies. More mountains lay ahead.

After stumbling out of the Bitterroots, the expedition entered Nez Percé territory. The Nez Percé fed them, and Chief Twisted Hair showed them how to make canoes. The expedition was able to travel swiftly down several rivers.

★ 6 ★

In March of 1806, the Corps of Discovery headed home. Sacagawea, Charbonneau, and their baby Pompey said good-bye at the Hidatsa–Mandan village. Often traveling 70 miles a day to reach home, the men met boats on the Missouri River, filled with American traders heading into the country's new land. When the expedition landed in St. Louis on September 23, 1806, everyone celebrated.

★ 8 ★

1806 MOUNTAIN MEN

BACKGROUND

Although the Lewis and Clark expedition traveled across the Rocky Mountains and reached the West Coast, their route was too difficult for wagons to travel. Mountain men such as Jedidiah S. Smith, James Bridger, James Beckwourth, and Thomas Fitzpatrick found passes through the western mountains that would allow wagon trains to travel to Oregon and California.

In 1822 William Henry Ashley placed an advertisement for "one hundred young men to ascend the Missouri River to its source, there to be employed for one, two, or three years." These men would work for the Rocky Mountain Fur Company trapping beaver, the material of choice for fashionable hats. There were three levels of trappers within the fur company: *engages*, who were given supplies and paid by the company; *skin trappers* or *share croppers*, who were given supplies by the company in return for a share of the pelts; and *free trappers*, who used their own supplies and kept all their profits. Between 1820 and 1830, about 1,000 mountain men trapped in the West.

A huge rendezvous was held each summer for the purpose of trading and selling the pelts. St. Louis merchants traveled into the West loaded with supplies, which cost the mountain men 200 to 1,000 percent above their normal prices. Native Americans were also encouraged to attend and trade.

When the beaver population in the West was nearly depleted, the market for pelts fell. Silk hats had become the rage. Many mountain men remained in the region and became guides for government expeditions and wagon trains or buffalo hunters. Their knowledge helped open the West to pioneer families.

IN FACT… The price of beaver pelts fell from a high of $6.00 per pound in the early 1830s to less than $3.00 per pound in 1843.

VOCABULARY

Introduce or review the following words: *expedition, wilderness, information, hired, including, pelts, rendezvous, transported, popular, grizzly, overland, blacksmith, stumble, fashion, partner, considered, performed, antelope, wrestled, mosquito, declined, battle, success, view, description.*

Before students begin to read, you may want to pronounce the names of people and places in the mini-book.

RESOURCES

BOOKS:
Jedidiah Smith and the Mountain Men of the American West
  by John Logan Allen (Chelsea House, 1991)
Mountain Men of the Frontier
  by Charles W. Sundling (Abdo and Daughter, 2000)

INTERNET:
42eXplore: Mountain Men
  http://www.42explore.com/mtnmen.htm
The Mountain Men: Pathfinders of the West 1810–1860
  http://xroads.virginia.edu/~hyper/HNS/Mtmen/home.html

ACTIVITIES

WHAT A CHARACTER! Many mountain men made their homes in the West, including Kit Carson and William Sherley Williams. Encourage students to find out about mountain men who are not mentioned in the mini-book. Then have them create their own mini-books about their subjects.

TALLER TALES: A combination of boredom and loneliness during the winter, socializing during the summer, and exciting events shaped some mountain men into great storytellers. Challenge students to hold their own rendezvous and swap tall tales about their adventures in their own environment.

WANTED: William H. Ashley's ad in a St. Louis newspaper persuaded many men to head West into lives of adventure. Ask students to think about what the lives of mountain men were really like, and what kind of characteristics someone would need to live that kind of life. Then have them write their own detailed want ads for mountain men and mountain women.

NATIVE AMERICANS AND THE MOUNTAIN MEN: Mountain men had contact, both friendly and unfriendly, with the Native Americans who lived in the West. Both groups integrated aspects of each other's culture into their own. Guide groups of students in researching the following tribes and their relationship with the mountain men: Crow, Nez Percé, Gros Ventre, Flathead, Blackfeet, and Cheyenne.

John Colter traveled west with the Lewis and Clark expedition. But he stayed behind to become a mountain man. Colter lived in the wilderness, trapping beavers and exploring.

William Henry Ashley used maps and other information from the Lewis and Clark expedition to set up his own fur trading company in the West. In 1822, Ashley hired more than a hundred young men as trappers.

★ 1 ★

The mountain men sold their pelts at a huge gathering called a *rendezvous*. They also bought or traded for more supplies, and swapped tall tales. Fur traders transported the pelts to St. Louis and other towns in the East by wagon. Hats made from beaver skin were popular in the U.S. and Europe.

★ 3 ★

Many famous mountain men worked for Ashley, including Jedidiah Smith, Jim Bridger, James Beckwourth, and Thomas Fitzpatrick. In the fall they trapped beaver in the mountains. They took a break during the winter, but would begin trapping again in the spring. In the summer they sold their pelts.

Jedidiah Smith (1799–1831) is perhaps the most famous of the mountain men. He rediscovered South Pass in the Rocky Mountains in Wyoming.

Smith was the first white American to cross the Mojave Desert to get to California. On his return, he crossed the Sierra Nevada Mountains and the Great Basin Desert. This was the first time Americans traveled overland to and from California.

James Bridger (1804–1881) started out as a blacksmith but then became a trapper. He was the first white man to stumble across the Great Salt Lake in Utah.

Beaver hats fell out of fashion in the 1840s. Like other mountain men, Bridger had to find other ways to make money. He and a partner built a fort along what would become the Oregon Trail.

★ 5 ★

Thomas Fitzpatrick (1799–1854) was attacked by Gros Ventre Indians on his way to a rendezvous. He rode his horse up a steep slope and then hid in a hole covered with brush. When the Indians left, Fitzpatrick began walking.

After the fur trade declined, Fitzpatrick became a scout and a guide. He helped guide the first wagon trains to Oregon and California.

★ 7 ★

James Beckwourth (1798–1866) was considered one of the best tall-tale tellers by mountain men. For six years, Beckwourth lived with the Crow. They gave him several names, based on brave acts he performed.

Like other mountain men, Beckwourth ran trading posts and acted as a guide. In 1848, he found a pass in Nevada. Beckwourth's Pass was later used by pioneers to reach California.

Mountain men guided John C. Frémont (1813–1890) into Oregon and California. His job was to make a map of the Oregon Trail. When Frémont returned home, his wife Jesse wrote his reports. They were a huge success! People in the East wanted to settle in the West.

1820 AMERICANS IN TEXAS

BACKGROUND

In 1820, Texas had three settlements—Nacogdoches in the east and the missions of San Antonio de Béxar and La Bahía del Espíritu Santo (Goliad) in the central part of the region. Spain, which controlled Mexico at that time, opened up Texas to foreigners. Mexican citizens were reluctant to settle in the area because of its remote location. After Mexico won its independence from Spain in 1821, it continued to allow immigration into Texas so that foreigners would spur the region's economic development and act as a buffer against Indian attacks and American encroachment.

Moses Austin hoped to make money by founding an American colony in Mexico. In 1821, Moses was granted permission for the colony, but he died a few months later. His son, Stephen F. Austin, continued his work and settled most of the "Old Three Hundred," the first 300 American families, in a colony along the Brazos, Colorado, and San Bernard Rivers by 1824. Farming families received one *labor* (about 177 acres) and ranching families got one *sitio* (about 4,428 acres).

Men who founded American colonies in Texas, such as Austin, were known as *empresarios*. They received land in exchange for settling families. They then sold that land to immigrants. Empresarios had administrative, judicial, and military responsibilities for their colonies.

Americans were drawn to Texas because inexpensive land was plentiful there. They also believed that the United States was about to buy eastern Texas from Mexico. If this happened, the value of their land would jump dramatically. As more Americans moved into Texas, their desire for self-government increased. War between Texians (white Americans who settled in Texas) and Mexico broke out in Gonzales in 1835. Santa Anna and his Mexican army were defeated at the Battle of San Jacinto in 1836. Sam Houston, the hero of San Jacinto, was elected president of the new republic.

IN FACT... In the 1820s, average land prices in the U.S. were $1.25 an acre. In Texas, land cost 4¢ an acre.

VOCABULARY

Introduce or review the following words: *colony, permission, governor, stubborn, site, settlers, gained, independence, government, colonists, sneak, citizens, obey, valuable, defend, responsible, brand, establishing, raid, sheriff, unfortunately, ignored, immigration, forts, soldiers, crazy, peaceful, demands, govern, arrested, jail, selected, volunteers, equipment, convince, defeated, independent, congratulations, voted.*

Before students begin to read, you may want to pronounce the names of people and places in the mini-book.

RESOURCES

BOOKS:
Legendary Texians
   by Joe Tom Davis (Eakin, 1982)
A Line in the Sand: The Alamo Diary of Lucinda Lawrence, Gonzales, Texas, 1836
   by Sherry Garland (Scholastic, 1998)
The Texas Sampler: Historic Recollections
   by Lisa Waller Rogers (Texas Tech University Press, 1998)

INTERNET:
The Handbook of Texas Online
   http://www.tsha.utexas.edu/handbook/online

ACTIVITIES

SIX FLAGS OVER TEXAS: Explain to students that the name for the well-known amusement park came from the fact that six different flags have been raised over Texas. Divide the class into six groups and have each group research the story of one of the six flags. They may bind their stories in a booklet that features the flags on the front cover.

PLAY THE TURTLE: Some Texians wanted to take advantage of the ups and downs of the Mexican political system so Texas could become more independent. Stephen F. Austin thought Texas should stay out of Mexico's business. He said, "Play the turtle, head and feet within our own shells." Ask students: Do you agree with Austin's words? In general, do you think it's better for a person or even a community to "play the turtle"?

I DON'T OWE YOU ANYTHING: One of the draws to living in Texas was that a person could leave his or her debts behind. Ask students: What do you think about this practice? Challenge them to take the point of view of one of the following people: an American who moved to Texas to get a new, debt-free start, or an American who is owed money by a Texian. Tell them to express their viewpoints in a newspaper editorial. You may want to bring in several issues of the editorial page of a local or state newspaper for students to study.

A COLONY IN CLASS: Remind students that the colonies in Texas were far from the Mexican capital. Stephen F. Austin and other colony founders were responsible for making sure that Mexican laws were obeyed and giving punishment if the laws were broken. Turn your class into a colony. Ask them to pretend that they are far away from the principal and teachers. Let students decide how to enforce existing school rules and to keep the classroom running smoothly.

American Moses Austin hoped to start a colony in Texas. At that time, 1820, Texas was part of Mexico. Austin went to San Antonio to ask permission to set up the colony.

Then Moses ran into an old friend, Baron de Bastrop, in San Antonio. The Baron also knew Governor Martínez. Moses's next meeting with the governor went much better.

★ 1 ★

Why did Americans want to move into Texas? They would get lots of land for only a little money. But they would have to become citizens of Mexico, not the United States, and obey Mexico's laws.

As head of the colony, Stephen F. Austin had to make sure everyone followed the laws. He also had to make sure the colony could defend itself against any kind of attack.

★ 3 ★

Moses Austin died soon after returning to the United States. His son, Stephen, took over plans for the Texas colony. Stephen found a site for the colony on the Brazos and Colorado Rivers. Soon American families began to arrive.

Why did Mexico decide to welcome American settlers? The country had just gained its independence from Spain. Nobody knew exactly what kind of government Mexico would have, or who would lead it.

★ 2 ★

Other men, Mexican and American, were also establishing colonies in Texas. Rancher Martín De León founded a Mexican colony and town on the Guadalupe River.

Green DeWitt, once an American sheriff, also got permission to settle on the Guadalupe River. Unfortunately, the Mexican government had given some of the same land to both men!

★ 4 ★

The forts and soldiers made many Texians angry. (Texians were white Americans who had settled in Texas.) They also didn't think that Mexico should stop more Americans from moving into Texas.

Texians held meetings in 1832 and 1833. They talked about what Mexico needed to do for Texas and Texians. Stephen F. Austin took the Texian's demands to Mexico City.

★ 6 ★

Stephen F. Austin was selected to find money, volunteers, and equipment for the war. He also tried to convince the U.S. government to make Texas a part of the United States.

Santa Anna defeated the Texians at the Alamo. But Texians led by Sam Houston beat the Mexican Army at the Battle of San Jacinto in 1836. Texas was now independent.

★ 8 ★

☙1838❧
TRAIL OF TEARS

BACKGROUND

In 1791, the Cherokee and the U.S. government signed the Treaty of Holston. The U.S. promised to protect Cherokee borders and to pay $1,000 a year for land that had been taken from them earlier. By the early 1800s, the Cherokee society was flourishing. In 1821, Sequoyah invented the Cherokee alphabet, and in 1827, the newspaper *Cherokee Phoenix* began publication in both Cherokee and English. The Cherokee built a nation with its own government.

When gold was discovered in Georgia in 1829, the state held a lottery for land. White settlers with winning numbers took over Cherokee land holdings. The Cherokee, led by Principal Chief John Ross, fought the takeover in the Supreme Court. In 1831, the Court ruled that the Cherokee Nation was a "dependent nation" and had to follow the laws of Georgia. Later, the Court reversed its ruling, saying that the Cherokee Nation was "a distinct community," and Georgia laws did not apply there. Meanwhile, President Andrew Jackson convinced Congress to pass the Indian Removal Act, which would force the southeastern tribes to move into Indian Territory west of the Mississippi River.

The Cherokee Nation was divided. Most wanted to stay in Georgia, but a small minority called the Treaty Party believed that they should move west before they lost everything. The Treaty Party secretly negotiated with the federal government to give up Cherokee land in Georgia for land in the West. Although only 20 Cherokee signed the treaty and 16,000 signed a petition opposing it, the treaty was declared valid. General Winfield Scott and his troops rounded up the Cherokees and placed them into stockades, where hundreds died from illness.

John Ross asked then-President Martin Van Buren to let him lead his people west. About 4,000 Cherokees—a quarter of those who set out—died on the trip. About 1,000 Cherokee escaped into the mountains of North Carolina. Today, they are known as the Eastern Band of the Cherokee.

IN FACT… The government allotted $65.88 for each Cherokee on the 1,000-mile trip to pay for food, supplies, and tolls.

VOCABULARY

Introduce or review the following words: *treaty, government, constitution, principal, supreme, Congress, declared, council, voted, territory, national, thunder, suffered, supplies, heartbroken.*

Before students begin to read, you may want to pronounce the names of people and places in the mini-book.

RESOURCES

BOOKS:
The Journal of Jesse Smoke: A Cherokee Boy, Trail of Tears, 1838
  by Joseph Bruchac (Scholastic, 2001)
The Cherokee (Indians of North America)
  by Theda Perdue (Chelsea House, 1989)
Cherokee Legends and the Trail of Tears
  by Tom Underwood (Cherokee Publications, 1997)

INTERNET:
A Brief History of the Trail of Tears
  http://www.cherokee.org/Culture/HistoryPage.asp?ID=2
The Trail of Tears in the Southeast Missouri Region
  http://www.rosecity.net/tears/trail/home.html

ACTIVITIES

THE CHEROKEE ALPHABET: In 1821, Sequoyah, with the help of his daughter Ahyokah, created a Cherokee alphabet. Each symbol in the alphabet represented a sound in Cherokee. Obtain a copy of the alphabet and a pronunciation guide from the library or Internet, and share it with students.

THE LEGEND OF THE CHEROKEE ROSE: The Cherokee Rose is the state flower of Georgia. Challenge individual or pairs of students to uncover the legend behind this flower and its connection to the Trail of Tears. Have them retell the legend in the form of a story, poem, song, or play.

THE DIFFERENT TRAILS: The Cherokee actually took three different overland routes and one water route. Guide students to find maps showing the different routes. The northernmost trail is the one considered by the Cherokee as the Trail of Tears. Ask groups to compare the routes and determine which one they would take. Set aside time for groups to share their decision-making processes and results with the rest of the class.

A TRAIL OF TEARS WEB SITE: Invite the whole class to collaborate on designing a Web site focusing on the Trail of Tears. Allow students to determine content areas and how to organize information in order to fill the page with text, images, and links.

The Cherokee people once lived in parts of Kentucky, West Virginia, Virginia, Tennessee, Alabama, North and South Carolina, and Georgia. As white settlers moved west, the Cherokees lost much of their land. Then they signed a treaty with the United States in 1791.

By 1827, the Cherokees had built schools, churches, and roads. They created the Cherokee Nation with its own government, laws, and constitution. John Ross was elected as the nation's Principal Chief.

⋆ 1 ⋆

President Andrew Jackson wanted to remove the Cherokee and other southeastern tribes from their land. He asked Congress to pass the Indian Removal Bill.

In 1830, Congress passed the Indian Removal Act and declared that the Cherokee and other tribes would have to move west of the Mississippi River. The Cherokee Nation was divided about what to do.

⋆ 3 ⋆

Then gold was discovered in Georgia. Even more white people poured into the state.

Georgia began to pass laws that hurt the Cherokee people. For instance, Cherokees couldn't dig for gold on their own land. Then Georgia decided to give away Cherokee land to white settlers.

★ 2 ★

A council meeting was held to decide what to do. A group called the Treaty Party wanted to work out a deal with the U.S. government. John Ross said he would do what the Cherokee people wanted him to do.

The Treaty Party went to Washington, D.C., anyway. They promised to turn over their land. In return, the U.S. government promised to pay $5 million to the Cherokee and give them land west of the Mississippi.

★ 4 ★

About 2,000 Cherokees moved into Indian Territory in what is today Oklahoma. But about 15,000 Cherokees remained in the East. The new president, Martin Van Buren, ordered the army to round them up.

The soldiers locked up the Cherokee people until they could be moved west. Many got sick, and hundreds died. Those who lived were crowded into boats.

The trip was a hard one. Supplies were low, and the weather was bad. Many people were still sick from being locked up. Everyone was heartbroken at having to leave home.

John Ross's wife, Quatie, died on the banks of the Mississippi River. About one out of every four Cherokees died on the trip west. They called the journey *nuna dat shun'yi*—"The Place Where They Cried."

Chief John Ross and the Cherokee National Council requested that the president put them in charge of moving their people to the West. President Van Buren agreed. On October 1, 1838, the Cherokees left their homes.

★ 6 ★

The 1,000-mile trip took between three and six months. John Ross led the last group of Cherokees into Fort Smith in Indian Territory in March 1839.

The Cherokee worked hard to become a strong nation again. They founded a capital and built schools. The nation was broken apart when Oklahoma became a state in 1907. But today, the Cherokee Nation is once again a strong force.

★ 8 ★

1843 OREGON TRAIL

BACKGROUND

Both the United States and England claimed the Oregon Country, which included present-day western Montana, Idaho, Oregon, Washington, and parts of Canada and Alaska. When American settlers who followed the Oregon Trail began flooding the Oregon Country in the 1840s, England focused its claim on the northern part of the region. In 1846, the Oregon Territory was claimed as part of the United States. In 1859, Oregon formally became a state.

Trappers and missionaries were the first groups to enter the Oregon Country. People responded to their stories of the region's fertile land and great forests. The first wagon train, consisting of about 1,000 settlers, left Independence, Missouri, in 1843. The trip to Oregon was 2,000 miles long and took from four to six months. In a few years, the trail became so crowded that people sometimes had to compete for good campsites at the end of the day.

The Oregon Trail meandered through Pawnee, Sioux, Cheyenne, Arapaho, Ute, Shoshone, Nez Percé, and Cayuse lands; however, only four percent of deaths along the trail were the result of confrontations with Native Americans. The majority of deaths were due to illnesses, such as cholera and smallpox, and accidents with guns. Relations between the American settlers and Native Americans became increasingly strained as resources along the trail disappeared—grasses were overgrazed, firewood was depleted, and buffalo were slaughtered.

Despite the fact that slavery was illegal in the Oregon Country, exclusion laws were enacted to keep out African Americans. Despite these laws, black pioneers such as George Washington Bush and Rose Jackson made their mark in the region.

The Oregon Trail was heavily traveled until the 1870s, when the Transcontinental Railroad became the favored means of transportation. The last wagon rolled down the Oregon Trail in 1912.

IN FACT... Estimates of the number of people who traveled on the Oregon Trail range from 80,000 to 200,000. About 10,000 people died on the journey.

VOCABULARY

Introduce or review the following words: *available, yoked, oxen, unexpected, progress, bacon, territory, pioneers, flooded, lightning, spooked, accidents, gunshots, bury, particularly, swept, condition, married, acres, rafts, barges, control, settled.*

Before students begin to read, you may want to pronounce the names of people and places in the mini-book.

RESOURCES

BOOKS:
The Oregon Trail
by Leonard Everett Fisher (Holiday House, 1990)
If You Traveled West in a Covered Wagon
by Ellen Levine (Scholastic, 1992)
A Frontier Fort on the Oregon Trail (Inside Story)
by Scott Steedman (Peter Bedrick Books, 1994)
Bound for Oregon
by Jean Van Leeuwen (Puffin, 1996)

INTERNET:
End of the Oregon Trail Association
http://www.endoftheoregontrail.org
The Oregon Trail
http://www.isu.edu/~trinmich/Oregontrail.html

ACTIVITIES

TRAIL RHYMES: Invite students to create their own poems about the Oregon Trail. To jumpstart their creativity, suggest they write an eleven-line poem. Each line of the poem will begin with a letter from the words OREGON TRAIL. For instance, line 1 would begin with the letter O, line 2 would begin with the letter R, and so on. You may want to let students collaborate on poems.

WHAT TO PACK? What if your class formed a wagon train to go down the Oregon Trail in 1844? Challenge students to use their minds creatively and practically to determine what kinds of supplies, equipment, and personal property they would take with them to their new homes in Oregon. Also have them determine how much of each item they would need for the entire journey; for example, how many pounds of flour would they need? Can they keep each wagon load under 2,000 pounds?

ON THE TRAIL: Wagon trains on the Oregon Trail passed landmarks such as Chimney Rock and the Craters of the Moon. Ask groups of students to draw maps showing the Oregon Trail. Have them include landmarks, rivers, forts, and other details they find interesting. For each location, they should write a brief description and/or find a photograph to include on the map. The Web sites listed at left will be helpful.

HOW MUCH FARTHER? How far do students typically walk in a day or a week? Work with the class in trying to determine everyone's daily and weekly mileage. Then ask students to calculate how long it would take them to walk the 2,000-mile-long Oregon Trail if they walked at their average daily rate.

In 1844 a wagon train guided by mountain man Moses Harris traveled on the Oregon Trail. Nathaniel Ford was the captain. George Washington Bush and his wife Isabel and their wagon were part of the train.

They left Independence, Missouri, in May when the grass was high. With any luck, they would travel the 2,000 miles to Oregon in four to six months.

⋆ **1** ⋆

Oxen were slow—they traveled only about two miles per hour. A wagon train could cover about fifteen miles a day. But, sometimes unexpected things happened that slowed down its progress.

⋆ **3** ⋆

The pioneers had to take enough food and supplies to last the entire trip. They also had to pack what they would need to live in the new territory. Some supplies were available along the trail, but prices were high.

The day started before sunup. The women cooked breakfast while the men yoked the oxen to the wagons. Then the wagon train moved out. Most people walked beside the wagons. They took an hour for lunch. Around six o'clock, they stopped for the night.

The beginning of the Oregon Trail passed through Cheyenne and Pawnee territory. Pioneers often traded with Native Americans for food. Native Americans also helped pioneers pull wagons out of the mud and rescue people from flooded rivers.

The real dangers on the Oregon Trail were sickness and accidents, such as gunshots and getting run over by wagons. One in ten pioneers died on the trail. George and Isabel took care of many children who lost their parents.

River crossings were probably the most dangerous events that people on the trail faced. They had to cross several rivers, including the Kansas, the North Platte, Green, and Columbia. The year 1844 was a particularly wet one, and the wagon train had to cross many swollen rivers.

⋆ **5** ⋆

Finally, the wagon train reached The Dalles. Here the wagons would float on rafts or barges down the Columbia River to Oregon City—the end of the trail.

John Minto returned from Fort Vancouver with supplies—and some news. George didn't like what he heard.

⋆ **7** ⋆

After traveling 1,554 miles, the wagon train reached Fort Boise. Like many other forts along the trail, Fort Boise began as a trading post.

Pioneers could stop at the fort to buy supplies and gather news about the condition of the trail ahead.

★ 6 ★

Most of the wagon train floated down the Columbia River. But George, his wife Isabel, and about 30 others moved north. They settled in a place that came to be known as Bush Prairie.

★ 8 ★

1849 CALIFORNIA GOLD RUSH

BACKGROUND

People like John Sutter had already begun to settle in California before gold was discovered. They had heard about California's favorable climate and fertile land. At that time, Mexico had claim to the territory. As more American settlers arrived, tensions increased between them and the Mexican ranchers. In June 1846, a group of Americans led the Bear Flag Revolt and declared that California was an independent republic. In 1848, as a result of the Mexican-American War, the U.S. gained possession of present-day California, Nevada, Utah, Arizona, and portions of New Mexico, Colorado, and Wyoming.

The discovery of gold on Sutter's land on the American River caused the population of California to swell. About 85,000 people had flooded into California by the end of 1849; they became known as Forty-Niners. Some took either the Oregon and California trails across the country, or the more southerly Santa Fe Trail. Others sailed from the Atlantic, crossed the Isthmus of Panama on foot or by horse, and then continued by boat on the Pacific Ocean. Another longer sea route took the miners around the tip of South America.

The Gold Rush helped turn San Francisco into a major city. Originally called Yerba Buena ("good herb" in Spanish), San Francisco became the port of entry for miners during the gold rush. Businesses sprang up to supply and equip the Forty-Niners. The small town of Sacramento also developed into a city thanks to the Gold Rush. In 1850, California became a state, and four years later, Sacramento was designated as its capital.

IN FACT... California was often called the "Go Ahead Country." People who flocked there were known as "go ahead people" because they had a sense of adventure and daring.

VOCABULARY

Introduce or review the following words: *hired, tend, sawmill, discovery, worst, pan, ruined, prospectors, government, claim, stew, cash, dangerous, nuggets, difficult, vein, consisted, attention.*

Before students begin to read, you may want to pronounce the names of people and places in the mini-book.

RESOURCES

BOOKS:
Seeds of Hope: The Gold Rush Diary of Susanna Fairchild, California Territory, 1849
  by Kristiana Gregory (Scholastic, 2001)
The Gold Rush
  by Bobbie Kalman (Crabtree Pub., 1999)
Gold Fever! Tales From the California Gold Rush
  by Rosalyn Schanzer (National Geographic Society, 1999)

INTERNET:
The Discovery of Gold in California
  http://www.sfmuseum.org/hist2/gold.html
PBS—About the Gold Rush
  http://www.pbs.org/goldrush/allabout.html

ACTIVITIES

WHATEVER HAPPENED TO...? This mini-book introduces John Sutter, John Marshall, and Sam Brannen to students. Ask students to find out what the final impact of the Gold Rush was on these men's lives. A good source is the PBS Web site, "New Perspectives on the West," http://www.pbs.org/weta/thewest/. Expand the activity to include other people, such as Levi Strauss, Lotta Crabtree, and the legendary figure, Joaquin Murieta.

GOING FOR THE GOLD: At first, gold could literally be picked up off the ground in California. But as gold became harder to find, prospectors developed new methods of mining. Have groups of students explore the various methods—placer mining, including panning; cradle mining; Long Tom mining; sluice mining; and hydraulic mining. Encourage them to display their findings in a variety of forms, including dioramas and diagrams.

CALIFORNIA, HERE I COME! People from the East could travel to California by land or by sea. Invite pairs of students to plan overland and sea routes from cities on the East Coast to California. Have them prepare maps showing their routes, and then decide which route they would prefer to take. Allow time for pairs to share their work with the rest of the class.

STAY HOME OR GO? Would students have joined the Gold Rush to California, or would they have remained at home? Have them write journal entries explaining their choices and how they arrived at their decisions.

John Sutter moved to California in 1839, when the region belonged to Mexico. Sutter built a fort and hired people to tend his crops and cattle. In 1847, he decided to build a sawmill.

On January 24, 1848, James Marshall spotted something shiny in the river. He picked up a piece of metal about the size of a pea. Looking closer at the river bottom, Marshall saw more pieces of metal.

⋆ **1** ⋆

Sam Brannen, a businessman from San Francisco, heard about the gold. He decided that gold was going to make him rich. But first, more people needed to know about the discovery.

Before running through the streets of San Francisco, Brannen bought every shovel he could find. Prospectors, people looking for gold, would need shovels and other supplies. Soon Brannen became the richest man in California.

⋆ **3** ⋆

Marshall hurried back to Sutter's Fort with his discovery. He and Sutter tested the metal in secret.

News about the gold leaked out. Almost all of Sutter's workers left to pan for gold in the American River. But the real gold rush hadn't begun yet.

★ 2 ★

People in the East heard about the gold in California, but didn't believe the news. In late 1848, President James Polk announced that the news was true. The California Gold Rush was on.

Fathers, brothers, and sons left their families and headed to California to strike it rich. After war between the United States and Mexico, California became part of the U.S. But in 1849, California had no real government or laws.

★ 4 ★

Women traveled to California, too. They washed and cooked for the miners. They also ran boarding houses where prospectors could stay. The women made more money than they did in the East.

Men arrived from all over the world—China, South America, Europe, Mexico, and Turkey. Like the Americans, they hoped to get rich and return home. But getting their gold home could be dangerous.

Many 49ers returned home without finding any gold at all. Others stayed in California and kept hoping they would strike it rich. They never did.

In 1348, about 300,000 Native Americans lived in California. That number dropped to about 50,000. Although Native Americans didn't care about gold, some miners didn't want them in the way.

People who went to California in search of gold were called Forty-Niners. Most of them arrived in 1849. But by the middle of the year, gold was harder to find. Others had already taken the nuggets of gold on the ground and in the rivers.

As gold became more difficult to find, the 49ers used different ways of mining. They changed the course of rivers to get to gold at the bottom. In 1853, they began turning huge flows of water on the riverbeds.

★ 6 ★

Before gold was discovered in California, San Francisco consisted of a handful of houses. Then James Marshall picked up the piece of gold in the American River, and everything changed. Almost overnight, San Francisco grew into a city. About 30 new houses were being built every day. The Gold Rush made Americans pay attention to California. In 1850, it became the 31st state.

★ 8 ★

1860 PONY EXPRESS

BACKGROUND

When the Pony Express began its operation on April 3, 1860, the United States was on the brink of Civil War. The threat of war made faster communication between California and the rest of the United States essential. Both the North and the South hoped that the western state would join their cause. The words and actions of newly elected President Abraham Lincoln would decide California. Instead of the average 21 days needed to deliver mail by steamship or stagecoach, the Pony Express brought news across the country in 9 or 10 days.

William H. Russell, William B. Waddell, and Alexander Majors, who started the Pony Express, were partners in a stage and freight line. They were under government contract to deliver supplies to the Army in the West. Hoping to gain a government contract to deliver the mail, Russell talked Waddell and Majors into forming "The Pony." Within two months, they had set up 156 stations, hired 120 riders and hundreds of other employees, and bought 400 horses.

Service ran between St. Joseph, Missouri, and Sacramento, California. Relays of riders on fast horses traveled along the Central Route, a distance of 1,966 miles. They carried letters written on thin tissue paper, which cost $5.00 per half ounce to send.

During its 19 months of operation, the Pony Express lost one rider and one bag of mail. The riders traveled a total of more than 650,000 miles. Unfortunately, the Pony Express lost money—about $200,000. Russell and his partners didn't obtain a government contract. The final blow to the Pony Express occurred when telegraph lines across the country were completed on October 24, 1861.

IN FACT... Riders promised not to swear, drink liquor, or fight with other Pony Express workers.

VOCABULARY

Introduce or review the following words: *mule, skinny, wiry, expert, risk, death, daily, orphans, telegrams, galloped, meanwhile, telegraph, business, reckon, leather, saddle, dangerous, territory, relief, occurred, sworn, inaugural, slavery, union, horrible, success, contract, government, worst, strung, scouts.*

Before students begin to read, you may want to pronounce the names of people and places in the mini-book.

RESOURCES

BOOKS:
The Pony Express
   by Peter Anderson (Children's Press, 1998)
Pony Express!
   by Steven Kroll (Scholastic, 2000)

INTERNET:
American West—Pony Express Information
   http://www.americanwest.com/trails/pages/ponyexp1.htm
Pony Express Home Station
   http://www.xphomestation.com

ACTIVITIES

WANTED: Read aloud the text of the want ad for Pony Express riders on page 2 of the mini-book. Tell students that the youngest rider was 11 years old, the oldest was in his 40s, and most riders were about 20 years old. Most of the riders were not orphans. They earned $100 a month. Ask students to think about whether or not they would have applied for the job. Then have those who are interested in the job write letters explaining why they should be hired. For those who are not interested in the job, have them write letters explaining why they are not.

RIDE EAST OR WEST: Challenge students to find the distance between their location and New York City or San Francisco, whichever city is farther away. Based on information given in the mini-book, about how long would it take them to ride Pony Express-style to that city? How many horses would they need in all? How many riders would the trip require? Assign this activity to groups of students.

STAMP OF APPROVAL: Display samples of commemorative postage stamps to students. You may want to visit the United States Postal Service Web site http://www.stampsonline.com. Discuss what each stamp celebrates and how the artist used graphic elements to pay tribute to the honoree. Then have students create their own commemorative postage stamps to celebrate the Pony Express. Display their work on the wall or compile them in a binder.

CHANGES IN COMMUNICATION: Discuss with students the impact that the construction of telegraph lines across the country had on the Pony Express. Then guide them in talking about other changes in communication technology and how these changes have affected people and industries. For instance, what impact is electronic mail having on mail delivered by planes, trucks, and people? Invite the class to work on a communications timeline.

If you had to mail a letter from New York to San Francisco in 1860, you could send it by steamship (and canoe and mule). It would arrive in 22 days. A letter traveling by wagon across the center of the United States would arrive in about 21 days. A letter sent by stagecoach across the southwestern United States would take about 21 days.

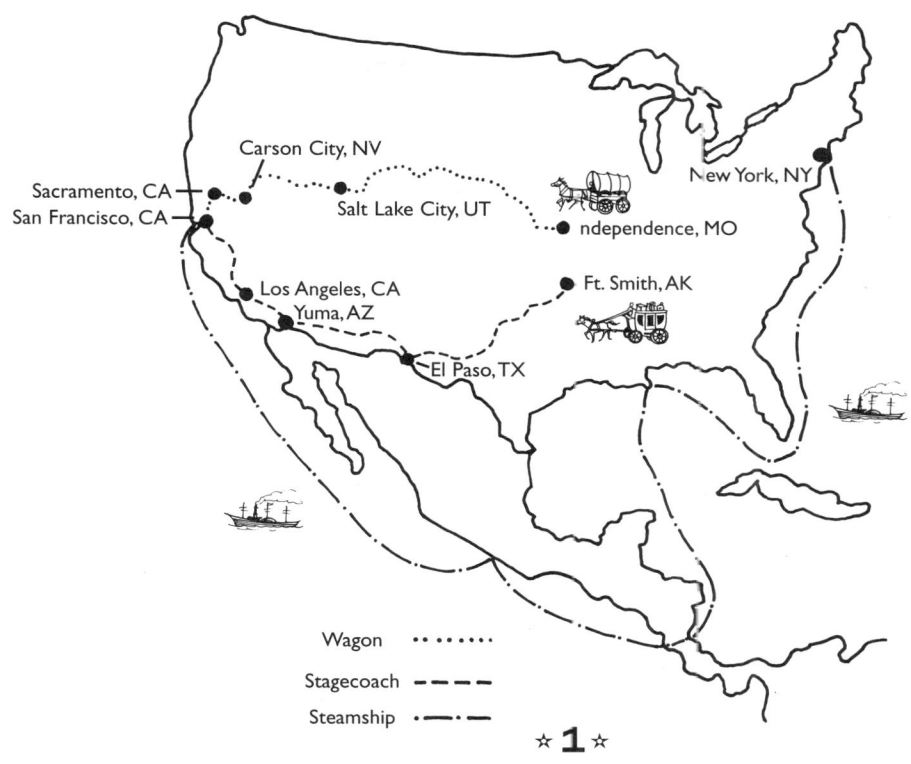

★ 1 ★

On April 3, 1860, the Pony Express began its first mail run.

That afternoon, in San Francisco, James Randall loaded the mail onto his horse. A crowd cheered as he rode east to Sacramento. James Randall carried 85 letters. Each letter cost $5.00 to send.

That evening, in St. Joseph, Missouri, Johnny Fry hopped on his horse and rode west. Johnny Fry carried 49 letters, five telegrams, and newspapers, which had arrived by train from New York and Washington, D.C.

★ 3 ★

William Russell, Alexander Major, and William Waddell decided that mail could be delivered faster. They dreamed up the Pony Express. Men on fast horses would carry mail from Independence, Missouri, to Sacramento, California—in 10 days!

The three men placed a want ad in the newspaper. Good riders and strong horses would be the most important part of the Pony Express.

2

On April 13, 1860, Sam Hamilton galloped into Sacramento and put the Pony Express mailbags on the boat for San Francisco. The mail from the East made it to California in just nine days!

Meanwhile, on the same day in St. Joseph, Missouri, the Pony Express brought in the mail from California.

4

How did the Pony Express deliver the mail so quickly? They hired almost 200 men and bought 400 horses. A rider rode about 75 to 100 miles. He got on a new horse every 10 to 15 miles—and he had two minutes to change horses.

Riders carried a leather bag called a *mochilla*, which had four locked boxes that held the mail. It fit easily over the specially made saddle and could be removed quickly. Together, the saddle and mochilla weighed only 13 pounds.

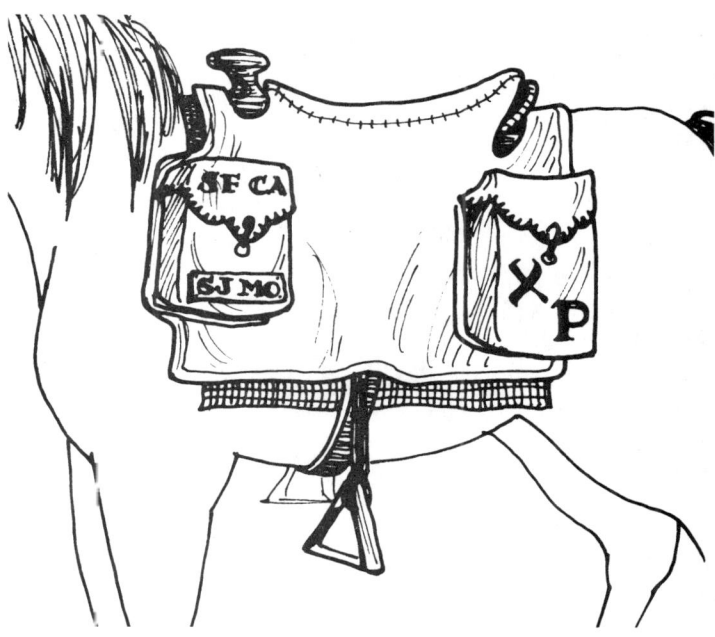

In 1861, the Pony Express brought Californians the news that the Civil War had begun at Fort Sumter in South Carolina. And the Pony Express delivered a secret message from a California man to President Lincoln.

Only once were riders unable to complete the trip. War had broken out with the Paiute Indians in Nevada.

Bill Cody (Buffalo Bill) made one of the longest trips in Pony Express history. He covered 322 miles of dangerous territory when his relief rider was killed. Jack Keetley rode 340 miles without stopping once.

The fastest Pony Express delivery occurred when Abraham Lincoln was sworn in as President. In only seven days and 17 hours, Lincoln's inaugural address reached California.

* 6 *

In many ways, the Pony Express was a success. But "The Pony" was losing money for its owners. They couldn't get a contract with the government to deliver the mail.

Then came the worst news: Telegraph lines had finally been strung clear across the country. People could send and receive telegrams from California. The last ride of the Pony Express was completed on November 21, 1861.

* 8 *

⇒1862⇐
HOMESTEADERS ON THE GREAT PLAINS

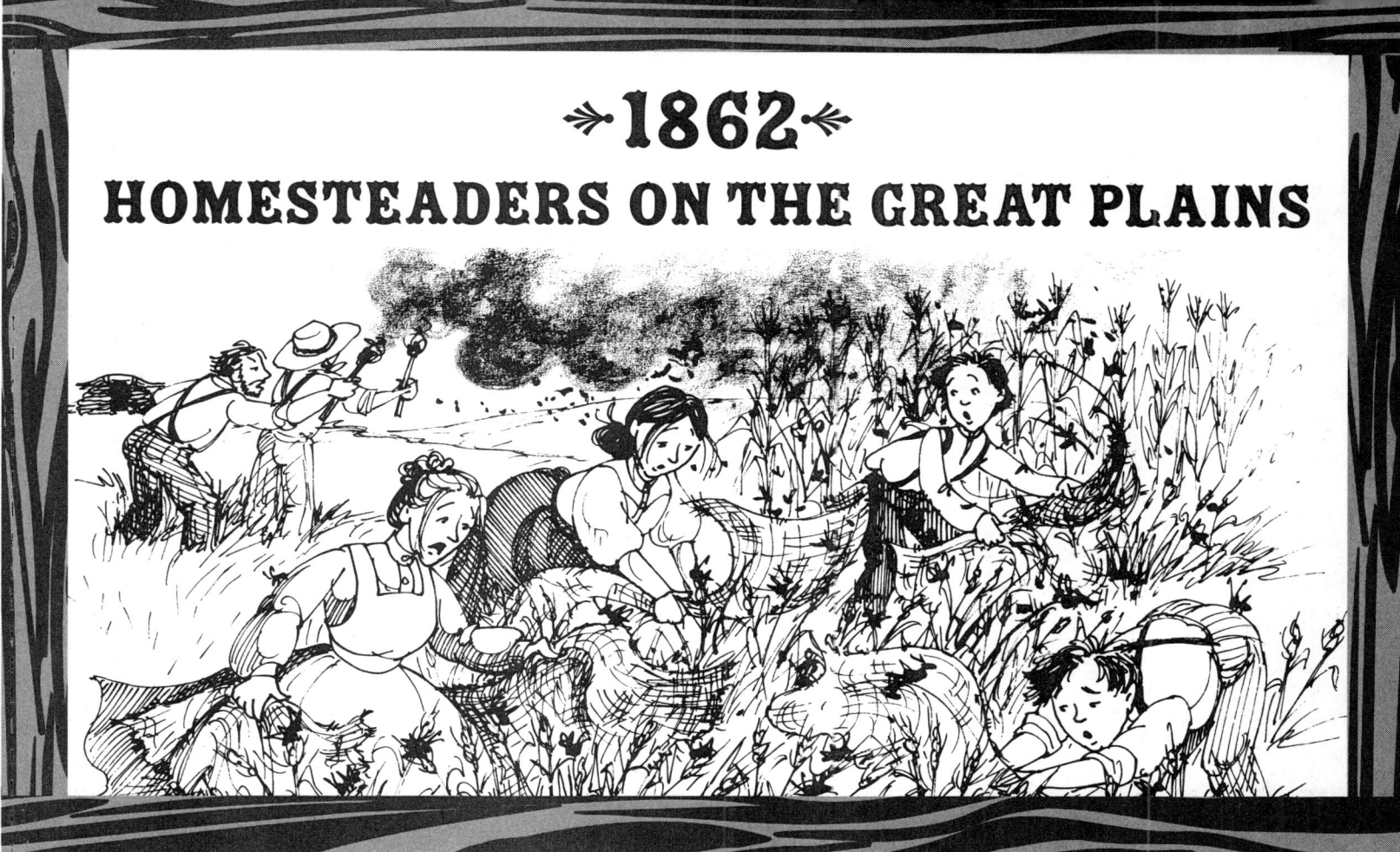

BACKGROUND

To ease overcrowding in the East and spur agricultural expansion in the West, Congress passed the Homestead Act of 1862. Any U.S. citizen—or person who was going to become one—over 21 years of age could get 160 acres of free public land. After paying a $10 fee, a homesteader had to live on the claim for at least six months out of every year for five years, and improve and cultivate the land. At the end of that period, the homesteader would "prove up" the claim and gain ownership of the land.

Women who were single, widowed, or divorced could claim land in their own names. The claims of married couples were placed in the husband's name. For the first time, it became possible for many lower- and middle-class women to possess land. Female members of the same family—daughters, sisters, nieces—often homesteaded on an acreage near their relatives. It was also common for women with children to sell their land in order to pay for their offspring's education.

Although hundreds of thousands of people took advantage of the Homestead Act, it wasn't entirely successful. The eastern United States remained crowded, and the dry climate beyond the 100th meridian wasn't conducive to farming. Due to the lack of water, most farmers needed more than 160 acres of land to be successful. The railroads also had snapped up most of the desirable land on the Great Plains and in the West. They did help spur growth, however, by conveying homesteaders west and then by transporting their crops to market.

The difficulties of farming on the Great Plains and in the West necessitated new methods of farming, such as dry farming, and the development of new and better tools, such as plows, barbed wire for fencing, and windmills.

IN FACT... More than 400,000 single people or families had applied for land under the Homestead Act by 1900.

VOCABULARY

Introduce or review the following words: *population, acres, citizens, improve, available, married, unfortunately, homesteaders, sod, prairie, celebrations, speeches, music, stalks, kernel, claim, newspaper, final, proof, proving, objected, officially.*

Before students begin to read, you may want to pronounce the names of people and places in the mini-book.

RESOURCES

BOOKS:
Prairie Songs
   by Pam Conrad (HarperCollins, 1987)
Stories from Where We Live—The Great North American Prairie
   by Sara St. Antoine (Milkweed Editions, 2001)
The Little House on the Prairie series
   by Laura Ingalls Wilder (HarperCollins)

INTERNET:
Adeline Hornbek and the Homestead Act– National Park Service
   http://www.cr.nps.gov/nr/twhp/wwwlps/lessons/67hornbek/67hornbek.htm
Land in Her Own Name
   http://www.lib.ndsu.nodak.edu/ndirs/exhibitions/pioneer/name/default.htm

ACTIVITIES

THE EXODUSTERS: The town of Nicodemus, Kansas, was founded in July 1877 by groups of African Americans from Kentucky. African-American settlers on the Great Plains were called Exodusters. Challenge groups of students to find out more about Exodusters and the communities they founded. Then have them create their own mini-books about Exodusters.

HOW MUCH IS 160 ACRES? One hundred sixty acres sounds like a lot of land, but is it? Guide the class in defining one acre. Then have them work together to find the equivalent of 160 acres on their school ground or another public place. They may also use a map in lieu of an actual location. Ask students: Do you think 160 acres is enough land on which to farm and build a house?

SPREAD THE WORD: Go over the requirements for owning land under the Homestead Act of 1862 that appear in the mini-book. Have students design a newspaper ad or poster that will spread the word about the act.

BARBED WIRE AND WINDMILLS: These two technological advances greatly affected the lives of farmers on the Great Plains. How have fencing and windmills continued to change? Ask pairs of students to research either barbed wire or windmills. They should briefly explain its impact on the Great Plains and then report on current advances, such as electronic fences or wind-powered energy.

In 1862, the Homestead Act was passed. The population in the East was growing. Congress and President Lincoln hoped people would move west and become farmers.

Many women were able to buy land for the first time because of the Homestead Act. Land was available to single women and women who were no longer married if they were the head of the family.

☆ 1 ☆

Winters on the Great Plains were long, hard, and lonely.

Neighbors did manage to get together for celebrations such as Christmas and the Fourth of July.

☆ 3 ☆

Unfortunately, there weren't many trees or much water on the Great Plains. Most of the best land had already been sold or taken by the railroads.

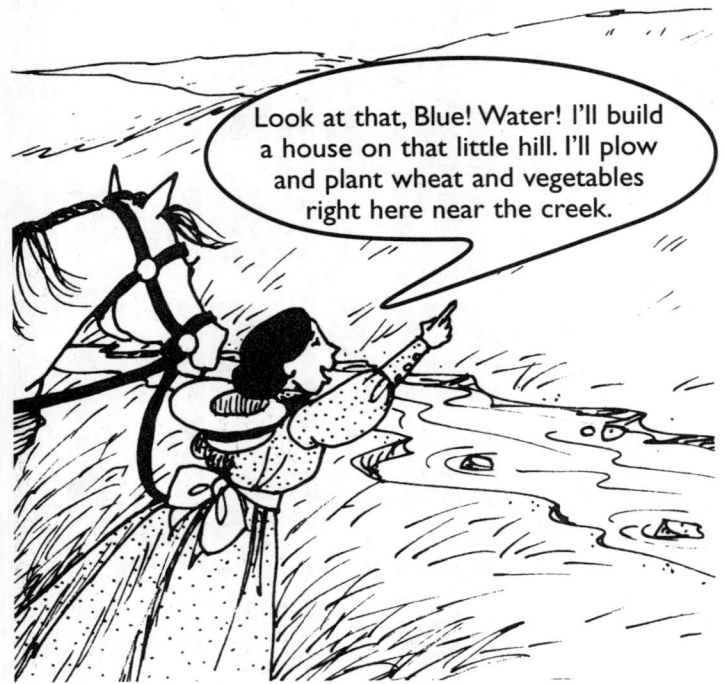

Homesteaders like Lucy Gaines built their houses out of sod. They cut pieces of sod out of the ground. The roots of prairie grasses in the sod made it strong. Sometimes the sod held surprises.

Like other homesteaders, Lucy had to take a job to earn enough money. She opened a school in her sod house. Other women worked in stores, took in sewing, or opened post offices in their homes.

Summers on the Great Plains could be hot and dry. If the prairie grass caught fire, flames would spread very quickly. Farmers searched their crops every day for signs of grasshoppers, which were hungry for tender young leaves and stalks.

I've never seen so many grasshoppers!

They'll eat every last leaf and kernel of corn!

If we don't stop those bugs here, they'll move on to your place next, Miss Gaines.

☆ 5 ☆

After living on the land for five years, a homesteader put an ad in the newspaper. This was called the "final proof" or "proving up."

You're the fourth woman homesteader I've seen this year.

You'll be seeing more women proving up soon.

If no one objected to the claim, then the land officially belonged to the homesteader.

Dear Ma and Pa, I am sending you a copy of my "final proof" ad. Nobody had anything to say against my claim. I own 160 acres of North Dakota! I miss you and wish you were closer, but I love my little piece of land. Love, Lucy

☆ 7 ☆

Lucy's neighbors included other homesteaders and Native Americans who lived in a nearby village. In her fourth year in North Dakota, Lucy decided to dig a well. It was hard work bringing water from the creek to her house.

★ 6 ★

The lack of water and trees on the Great Plains changed the way farmers did things. New inventions such as barbed wire and better windmills helped them.

Women homesteaders ranged in age from their early 20s to their 60s. They came from many different backgrounds—white and black Americans, Jewish and Arab women, and Europeans from Germany and Scandinavia.

★ 8 ★

1866 CATTLE DRIVES

BACKGROUND

The great cattle drives occurred between 1866 and 1890. By the end of the Civil War, the cattle supply east of the Mississippi River had been exhausted. In Texas, because of the war and a shortage of labor, cattle roamed freely. Texans returning home from the war decided to round up a herd and drive it to a market, where they could get $40 to $60 a head.

Texans had their choice of several trails and markets. Cattle buyer Joseph McCoy brought cattle up the Chisholm Trail. He built cattle pens and a hotel at the railhead in Abilene, Kansas. Then McCoy had surveyors find a route south to Texas. For 220 miles, the route followed Jesse Chisholm's road to his trading post on the Canadian River. Other Texans drove their herds up the Shawnee Trail to Kansas City or Sedalia, Missouri. The cattle were shipped from there to Chicago meatpackers. Cattlemen Charles Goodnight and Oliver Loving blazed the Goodnight-Loving Trail from Texas northwest to the Colorado gold mines.

A typical herd consisted of 3,000 cattle and 11 individuals. Trail bosses in their 20s usually made about $100 a month. Other cowboys, called *waddies*, ranged in age from 12 to 18 years old and earned between $25 and $40 a month. Cooks could make $75 a month. Wranglers in charge of the *remuda*, or stable of extra horses, were paid about $50 a month. The trip to market could take six weeks. The cattle were driven only 10 to 15 miles a day so they could graze and remain fat.

Cattle drives ended with the fencing of land and the quarantines placed on Texas cattle by several states, including Kansas and Missouri. Longhorns carried a tick that caused Texas fever or Spanish fever, which affected domestic cattle along the trails. Texas cattlemen then began to round up their cattle, take them to the nearest railhead, and send them to market by rail.

IN FACT... The Cowboy Hall of Fame opened in Oklahoma City in 1965. The museum overlooks the Chisholm Trail. The Cowgirl Hall of Fame is located in Forth Worth, Texas.

VOCABULARY

Introduce or review the following words: *stew, unbranded, roamed, dogies, advice, further, breathing, restless, reservation, destroys, folks, stampedes, stampeding, surrounded, exchanged, wrist, upstream, wounds, partner, acres, graze.*

Before students begin to read, you may want to pronounce the names of people and places in the mini-book.

RESOURCES

BOOKS:

Wrango
   by Brian Burk (Harcourt, 1999)

The Journal of Joshua Loper: A Black Cowboy
   by Walter Dean Myers (Scholastic, 1999)

Get Along, Little Dogies: The Chisholm Trail Diary of Hallie Lou Wells: South Texas 1878
   by Lisa Walker Rogers (Texas Tech University Press, 2001)

INTERNET:
Trail Drives of the Old West
   http://www.net.westhost.com/trail1.htm

ACTIVITIES

ON THE TRAIL: Have groups of students research cattle trails such as the Chisholm, Shawnee, or Western Trails. Ask them to use their research to collaborate on a mini-book about that trail.

A DAY IN THE LIFE OF A COWBOY: Cattle driving was anything but glamorous for a cowboy. He (or she) endured heat, dust, rain, stampedes, and boredom for little pay. (Girls disguised themselves as boys to join cattle drives.) Challenge students to find out about a typical day in the life of a cowboy on a cattle drive. They should learn the day's routine, what cowboys wore and ate, and what surprises and disasters could occur. Suggest they write journal entries to depict a day or more in the life of a cowboy.

WHERE DOES YOUR HAMBURGER COME FROM?
Cattle drives ended in the 1880s with the fencing of land along the trails and state quarantines placed on Texas cattle. Pose the following question for pairs of students to research: How does beef get to your table today?

AROUND THE CAMPFIRE: After a long day on the trail, cowboys would gather around the campfire and entertain each other with stories and songs. Hold a campfire gathering in your classroom. Encourage students to contribute their own stories and songs about a cowboy's life. They may also bring in existing songs and stories they have found.

After the Civil War, the North was low on cattle. Almost all the cattle had been killed to feed the Northern people and the Union army.

Texas, however, was filled with cattle. More than 3 million longhorns and wild, unbranded cattle roamed the state. Men like Charles Goodnight helped round up most of the cattle in the state.

★ 1 ★

A cattle drive started with the cook who drove the chuck wagon. Horse wranglers herded a *remuda* of extra horses behind him. The trail boss and his top hand rode "point" beside the head of the herd. Further back, more cowboys traveled on either side of the herd. Bringing up the rear were the youngest cowboys, called the "drags."

★ 3 ★

Charles Goodnight planned to sell his herd of cattle in Colorado. Gold had been discovered there. People would be willing to pay a lot of money for his herd. Then one day Goodnight met Oliver Loving.

Loving was a rancher. He knew about cattle and about cattle driving. He decided to go on the trail with Goodnight. The two men made a good team.

2

Goodnight and Loving left Belknap, Texas, on June 6, 1866 with 2,000 cattle and 18 men. Goodnight rode ahead to search for water, grass, and Indians. Loving managed the cattle and cowboys.

At the end of the first day, the cattle were thirsty and restless. Goodnight decided to push hard to reach the Pecos River. Nobody slept for three days as the herd moved west. Then the cattle smelled the river and rushed toward the water.

4

They lost a hundred cows. At Fort Sumner, New Mexico, they stopped at a reservation where the U.S. Army held more than 8,000 Navajo Indians. The army bought most of the cattle for $12,000 in gold.

Goodnight and Loving drove another herd to Fort Sumner and sold it to the army. Then they headed back to Texas to set up another cattle drive to New Mexico.

★ 5 ★

Loving and Bill found a place to hide, but the Indians quickly surrounded them. The Comanche took the men's horses. Both sides exchanged shots. Loving was hit in his wrist and his side.

Loving told Bill to go back to the cattle drive to tell them what had happened. Under the cover of darkness, Bill slipped off. He left six guns with Loving.

★ 7 ★

The Comanche had also heard about the cattle drives. They tried to steal the cattle by starting stampedes. Goodnight was worried they wouldn't reach New Mexico in time to sell their cattle to the army.

For several days, Loving and One-Armed Bill rode at night. They didn't see any Indians. Loving decided to take a chance and ride in the daylight. That was a mistake.

* 6 *

When Goodnight and his men reached the river, Loving was gone. Loving thought Bill had been killed so he made his way upstream. People passing by found Loving and took him to Fort Sumner.

In less than a month, Loving died of his wounds. Goodnight took his partner's body back to Texas along the Goodnight-Loving Trail. The trail became one of the most important trails in the Southwest.

* 8 *

1869
TRANSCONTINENTAL RAILROAD

BACKGROUND

The construction of the transcontinental railroad from Omaha, Nebraska, to Sacramento, California, spanned six years and required the labor of 20,000 workers, most of whom came from China and Ireland. The transcontinental railroad sped travel and communication across the United States, helped settle and develop the country's interior, advanced trade and other industries, and was crucial to national defense.

After the South seceded, Congress was able to pass the Pacific Railway Act of 1862, which specified a northern route for the railroad—something Southern congressmen had opposed. Two new railroad companies were created, the Central Pacific Railroad (CPRR) and the Union Pacific Railroad (UPRR). The CPRR would build to the East, and the UPRR would build to the West. The government loaned the companies $16,000 for each mile of track laid across the plains, $32,000 for each mile laid across the Great Basin, and $48,000 for each mile laid in the mountains. They also received public lands—a total of 33 million acres—on either side of the tracks laid.

Both railroads faced many challenges. The Central Pacific workers had to blast and drill through the Sierra Nevada Mountains and endure blizzards. Wood for ties was available, but rails, engines, wheels, and other equipment had to be ordered from the East. Supplies were shipped around South America, an expensive and dangerous trip of 18,000 miles. Supplies for the UPRR crew had to be shipped up the Missouri River and then transported to the construction site by special trains, often up to 40 cars long. The UPRR faced a shortage of wood in the Great Plains.

When the two railroads met in Promontory Point, Utah, the CPRR line was 742 miles long and the UPRR was 1,032 miles.

IN FACT... Each rail weighed 700 pounds and was about 10 to 12.5 yards long. Each mile of track contained between 2,260 and 2,640 wooden ties.

VOCABULARY

Introduce or review the following words: *discovery, transportation, communications, engineer, approve, threatening, civil, soldiers, troops, public, steel, construction, fuel, equipment, drill, solid, blizzards, powder, explodes, recently, shelter, problems, solved, spikes, crew, ceremony, kidnapped, owe, completion, telegraph.*

Before students begin to read, you may want to pronounce the names of people and places in the mini-book.

RESOURCES

BOOKS:
Full Steam Ahead
  by Rhoda Blumburg (National Geographic Society, 1996)
The Journal of Sean Sullivan: Transcontinental Railroad Worker
  by William Durbin (Scholastic, 1999)
Ten Mile Day
  by Mary Ann Fraser (Henry Holt, 1996)

INTERNET:
Central Pacific Railroad Photographic History Museum
  http://cprr.org
Union Pacific – History and Photos
  http://www.uprr.com/aboutup/history

ACTIVITIES

WHAT HAPPENED TO THEODORE JUDAH? Ask students to find out what happened to one of the most important men behind the transcontinental railroad. (On his way to the East Coast, traveling across the Isthmus of Panama, Judah contracted yellow fever. He died soon after in New York City.) Introduce the word *irony* to your class. How does the word apply to Judah's situation? As an alternative, have students research the life of one of the Big Four: Leland Stanford, Collis Huntington, Mark Hopkins, and Charles Crocker.

RAILROAD JOURNEYS: What are your students' experiences with long or short journeys by train? Have them write their experiences in a travel diary, with illustrations. If students haven't traveled by train, discuss the fact that the U.S. government provides monetary support to Amtrak. Ask students: Is a passenger train system necessary in this country? Should Americans be asked to support it with their tax dollars?

TRANSPORTATION TODAY: Given the various forms of transportation available today, how would students choose to travel across the United States? Challenge groups of students to plan transcontinental trips. They may begin their trips on either coast, but they must end on the opposite coast. Provide atlases and bus, airline, and train schedules (either printed or online) for groups to use in developing their itineraries.

TRAINS, TRAINS, TRAINS: Let students follow their own interests in researching aspects of trains. They may consider any topic, such as how railroads are built, the history of trains, what a typical freight train may carry, bullet trains, and so on. Pair or group students who have similar interests. Hold a Train Appreciation Day in your classroom. Invite other classes to visit and learn all about trains.

Before 1850, most people traveled by water or on highways. That's how they shipped goods and supplies, too. Then railroads built in the East began to carry more passengers and goods.

The discovery of gold in California and silver in Nevada changed the way Americans thought about transportation. Moving people, supplies, and communications quickly across the nation became important.

⋆ 1 ⋆

The Pacific Railway Act of 1862 declared that the Union Pacific Railroad was to build from the East to the West. The starting point would be Omaha, Nebraska.

The Central Pacific Railroad built the railroad from west to east, starting at Sacramento, California. Leland Stanford, Collis Huntington, Mark Hopkins, and Charles Crocker headed the Central Pacific. They had made lots of money during the Gold Rush by selling supplies to miners.

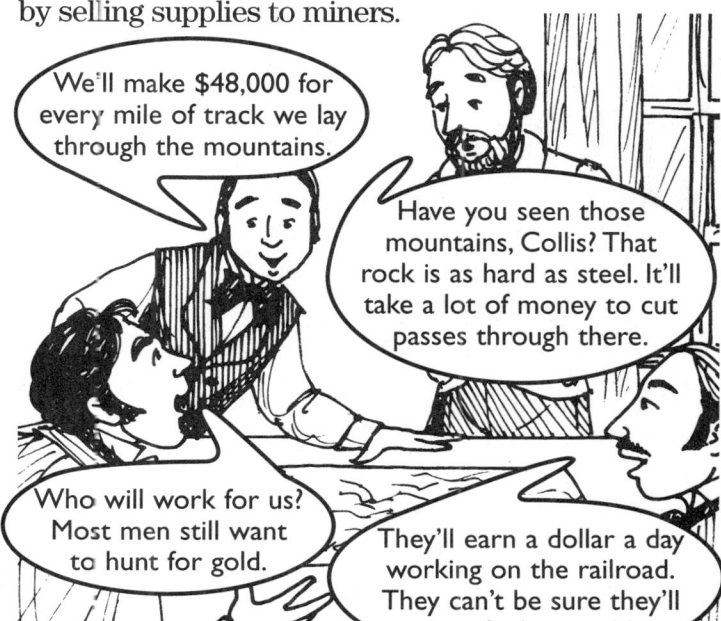

⋆ 3 ⋆

Theodore Judah, a railroad engineer, wanted to build a railroad across the United States. He planned a route from the West to the East. Judah tried to get Congress to approve his plan for a transcontinental railroad.

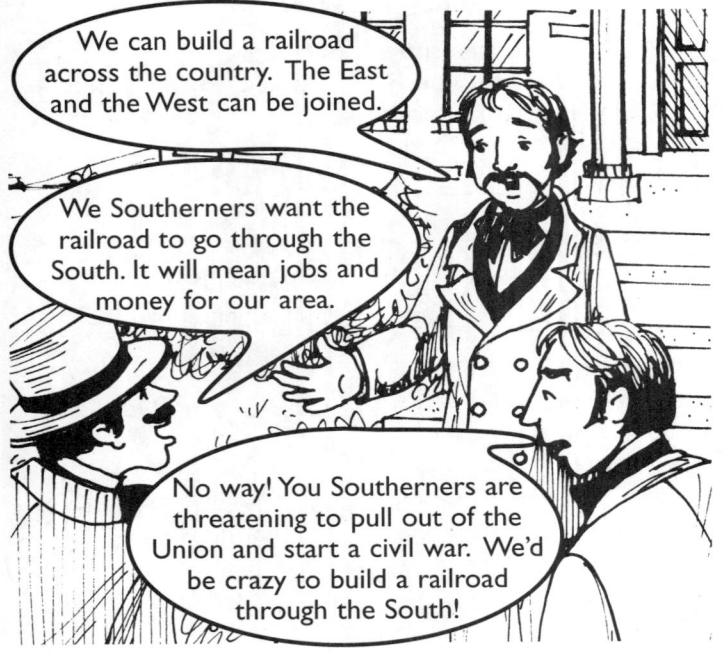

Civil War broke out. The North decided to build the transcontinental railroad. It was important to keep California in the Union. The railroad would make it possible to supply the West with soldiers and supplies.

✯ **2** ✯

After two years, the Union Pacific Railroad had laid only 40 miles of track. The Union Pacific decided to hire Grenville Dodge to take over the construction of the railroad.

Dodge had a hard job ahead of him. A railroad needs lots of trees to make railroad ties. There weren't many trees on the Great Plains. And food, supplies, fuel, and equipment had to be brought in from the Missouri River.

✯ **4** ✯

One of the biggest problems the Central Pacific faced was the Sierra Nevada Mountains. Workers had to drill and blast tunnels through miles of solid rock.

In winter, blizzards dropped several feet of snow on the tracks. Workers had to build wooden sheds over the tracks so they could work.

When workers kept quitting, Charles Crocker hired Chinese workers. They worked long and hard—and for less money than other workers.

On April 28, 1869, Union Pacific and Central Pacific workers raced to see who could lay the most track in one day. All day, the men laid the rails, set the ties, and hammered in the spikes. When it was over, Central Pacific had won. They had laid 10 miles of track in 12 hours. Nobody has ever broken that record.

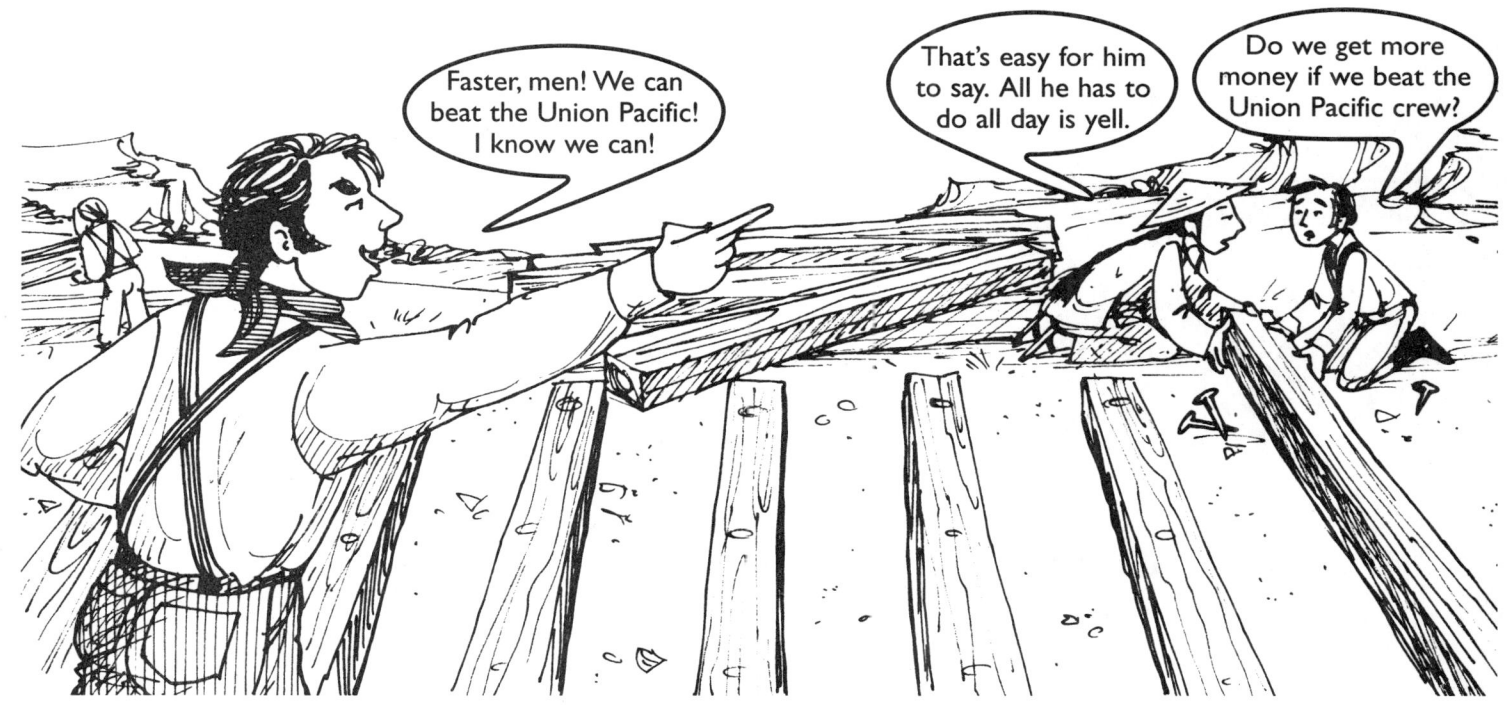

Union Pacific workers were mostly Irish men who had recently come to the United States. Other workers were men who had served in the Civil War. They worked seven days a week, 12 to 16 hours a day.

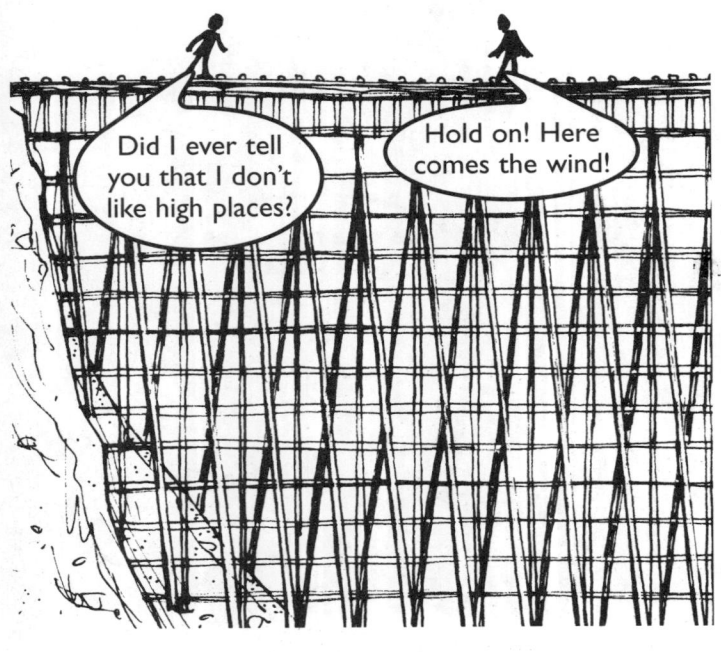

Native Americans weren't pleased to see the railroad being built through their hunting grounds. They attacked the railroad and workers. Dodge sent for General William T. Sherman to handle the Indians.

★ 6 ★

The two railroads were due to meet at Promontory Point in Utah in early May. On his way to the ceremony, Thomas Durant, vice president of the Union Pacific, was kidnapped by angry workers.

The workers got their pay and let Durant go on to Promontory Point.

The Union Pacific and Central Pacific trains slowly nosed toward each other. Leland Stanford was supposed to tap a golden spike into the rails. He missed. Durant was supposed to tap a silver spike into the rails. He missed, too. News of the completion of the railroad went out by telegraph all over the nation.

★ 8 ★

1886
GERONIMO AND THE CLOSING OF THE WEST

BACKGROUND

With the end of the Civil War, the United States turned its military attention to the Native American tribes that ranged across the Great Plains. Prospectors hungry for gold and silver moved from west to east, while settlers and railroad builders continued their westward migration. The Native Americans stood in the way. And they were increasingly concerned about the loss of resources to white Americans.

William Tecumseh Sherman and Philip Sheridan, both Union generals in the Civil War, led the military campaign against the Indian tribes. They wanted Native Americans contained on reservations. To accomplish this, Sheridan initiated surprise attacks on Indian villages in the winter. Despite the overwhelming numbers of soldiers arrayed against them, Native American leaders such as Chief Joseph, Red Cloud, and Geronimo managed to escape capture for a time.

Apache raiding parties traditionally attacked their neighbors, whether they were other Native American groups or white or Mexican settlers. When the medicine man Geronimo returned from an Apache raiding party in Mexico, he found that Mexican soldiers had killed his mother, wife, and young children. When the Apache were forced onto the San Carlos Reservation in Arizona 1875, Geronimo escaped twice with groups of men, women, and children. Captured for the last time in 1886, Geronimo and his band were exiled to Florida as prisoners of war. Geronimo, still a captive of America, died in Oklahoma in 1909.

By the end of the 19th century, the American frontier—the region of the country that was unsettled or undeveloped—no longer existed. Using a standard of six people per square mile, the 1890 U.S. Census declared that the American frontier was closed.

IN FACT... Geronimo's real name was Goyathlay or "One who yawns." He may have gotten the name Geronimo from Mexican soldiers after an Apache raid that took place on the Feast of St. Jerome.

VOCABULARY

Introduce or review the following words: *fought, protecting, forts, region, shelter, control, treaty, reservation, troops, freedom, medicine, bullets, future, scouts, harsh, captured, warriors, citizens, agreed, surrendering, agree, suggest, business, choice, dangerous, government, livestock, prisoner.*

Before students begin to read, you may want to pronounce the names of people and places in the mini-book.

RESOURCES

BOOKS:

The Apaches
 by Virginia Driving Hawk Sneve (Holiday House, 1997)

Geronimo: Apache Freedom Fighter
 by Spring Hermann (Enslow, 1997)

Geronimo
 by William Thompson (Chelsea House, 2001)

INTERNET:

Geronimo: His Own Story
 http://odur.let.rug.nl/~usa/B/geronimo/geroni17.htm

ACTIVITIES

NATIVE AMERICAN LEADERS: Ask groups of students to research the lives of the Native American leaders who fought against being placed on reservations; for example, Red Cloud, Chief Joseph, Sitting Bull, Crazy Horse, Black Kettle, and Quanah Parker. Also suggest that a group study Tecumseh, after whom General Sherman was named. Then have students design an encyclopedia page or a Web page to display their findings.

THE BUFFALO COMMONS: Today some counties in the Great Plains have less than two people per square mile. People have suggested turning the Great Plains into a "buffalo commons." Buffalo would be able to wander freely and unfenced. Communities would be able to use fences to keep out buffalo but not to keep them in. Ask students to write newspaper editorials either for or against the buffalo commons proposal.

OKLAHOMA LAND RUSH: The General Allotment Act of 1887 granted 160 acres of reservation land to heads of Indian households. The act was designed to encourage Native Americans to become individual farmers and ranchers. The remaining reservation land was made available to white settlers. At noon on April 22, 1889, 2 million acres of Indian Territory were opened up to white settlers. Have students research the Oklahoma Land Rush. Suggest topics such as The Sooners and the founding of Guthrie, Kingfisher, and/or Oklahoma City. Let students design historical markers or create mini-books to present their findings.

NEW FRONTIERS: Ask students to envision a time when they might become pioneers. Challenge them to think about the future and how it might impact their lives. What characteristics do they possess that would help them succeed as pioneers? Ask students to write brief essays about their pioneering futures. After they share their essays with the rest of the class, suggest that students put their work in time capsules at home. Encourage them to include material about past and present pioneers they admire.

General William Tecumseh Sherman fought for the Union during the Civil War. After the war, he was put in charge of protecting the land from the Mississippi River to the Rocky Mountains. He built army forts across the region.

General Philip Sheridan served under Sherman. Sheridan came up with a plan to control the Plains Indians. He wanted to attack the tribes in their villages during the winter.

★ 1 ★

In 1875, all Apaches west of the Rio Grande were forced onto the San Carlos Reservation in Arizona. The group included Geronimo, an Apache medicine man known for his wisdom.

Years before, Mexican soldiers had killed Geronimo's mother, wife, and three young children. After that, Geronimo led as many raiding parties as he could.

★ 3 ★

In 1868, Sherman and Chief Red Cloud signed a treaty. The Lakota received land, including the Black Hills. But when gold was discovered in the Black Hills, the U.S. took back the land. Ten years later the Lakota were living on a reservation.

Also in 1868, U.S. troops rounded up the Kiowa, Comanche, Arapaho, and Cheyenne in Oklahoma and placed them on reservations. Southern Plains Indians lost their freedom in 1875. Northern Plains Indians lost theirs in 1877.

Geronimo led other Apaches off the reservation in 1882. General George Crook used Apache scouts to help track them down. They were captured and returned to San Carlos.

Geronimo didn't stay on the reservation for long. In 1885, he escaped again with Chief Juh, 35 warriors, and more than 100 women and children.

More than 5,000 soldiers, 500 Apache scouts, and many white citizens chased after Geronimo. Finally Geronimo agreed to talk to General Crook about surrendering.

President Grover Cleveland and General Phil Sheridan were angry with Crook. They didn't want Geronimo and his Apaches to ever return to the reservation.

★ 5 ★

On September 3, 1886, Geronimo and the Apaches met General Miles in Skeleton Canyon. They gave themselves up.

A few days later, Geronimo and his people—including many Apache scouts who had worked for the U.S. Army—were loaded onto a train.

★ 7 ★

Miles sent guards to waterholes and mountain passes, and soldiers to the tops of mountains. The soldiers used mirrors to signal one another. Miles also fired all the Apache scouts.

In July of 1886, Geronimo and his people decided to give themselves up. They learned that they would be sent to Florida with their families. They would probably never be able to return to Arizona.

★ 6 ★

After Geronimo arrived at Fort Pickens in Florida, he didn't see his family for two years. He and other warriors worked everyday, sawing logs.

Geronimo and his family were next moved to Fort Sill in Oklahoma. The U.S. government built them houses and gave them livestock to raise. When Geronimo died in 1909, he was still a prisoner.

★ 8 ★